DEDICATION

We dedicate this book to Soot Zimmer, whose vibrant personality, unending love, and caring support facilitated the success of Don Zimmer's family life and baseball career. Her countless efforts to preserve sixty-six years of treasured baseball memories are the essence of this book.

ABOUT THE AUTHORS

Cathy Pappalardo and Judy Newcomb are retired teachers who feel compelled and privileged to share insights from the life of baseball's legendary Don Zimmer. The italicized words in this book are meant to enrich the readers' vocabularies and to challenge them to exemplify these qualities in everyday life.

Live life inspired !
Cathy Pappalardo
&
Judy Newcomb

ACKNOWLEDGMENTS

Our enormous thanks to Soot Zimmer for donating special pictures from her treasured collection. We appreciate the input from the Zimmer family, and we are grateful to them for allowing us to share their precious memories through this picture book.

www.mascotbooks.com

Inspiration from Legendary Zim

For more information, please contact:
Mascot Books
620 Herndon Parkway, Suite 320
Herndon, VA 20170
info@mascotbooks.com

Library of Congress Control Number: 2021908842

CPSIA Code: PRT0621A

ISBN-13: 978-1-63755-012-0

Printed in the United States

INSPIRATION FROM
LEGENDARY ZIM

CATHY PAPPALARDO *and* JUDY NEWCOMB

Don Zimmer had one of the longest careers in Major League Baseball. He was part of the game for sixty-six years. His love of baseball began at the age of eight, when his dad gave him his first glove and introduced him to America's Pastime.

Don Zimmer is third from the left in the bottom row of his Knot Hole Baseball team picture. (The term Little League did not exist in those days.)

Don played many sports in high school. His American Legion Baseball team became National Champions, and the players were congratulated by the legendary Babe Ruth.

Babe Ruth is seen shaking the hands of the American Legion team.

Many people have *nicknames*. The Zimmer family had several. Some people shortened Don Zimmer's name and called him Zim. The famous Roy Campanella nicknamed him Popeye after Zim hit two homeruns in one game. Campi felt Zim's muscular arm and remarked, "You have muscles like Popeye!"

 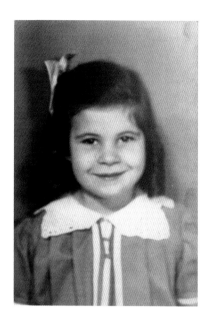

Don Zimmer's wife, Jean Carol, who was his high school sweetheart, was known as Soot, which was short for Sootala. This was a term of endearment given to her by her grandmother, whose ancestors were from Germany.

Brooklyn Dodger players Jackie Robinson, Zim, Duke Snider, and Roy Campanella

Zim is playing second base for the Los Angeles Dodgers, and he is turning a double play.

In 1949, at the age of eighteen, Zim was offered a professional baseball contract with the Brooklyn Dodgers. One of his teammates was the legendary Jackie Robinson. The Dodgers won the World Series Championship in 1955.

Zim played for the Brooklyn Dodgers, the Los Angeles Dodgers, the Chicago Cubs, the New York Mets, the Cincinnati Reds, and the Washington Senators. He finished his playing career with the Toei Fliers in Tokyo, Japan.

In 1962, Zim was the first player to wear the New York Mets uniform.

Zim coached or managed a number of teams: the Montreal Expos, the San Diego Padres, the San Francisco Giants, the Chicago Cubs, the Boston Red Sox, the Colorado Rockies, the Texas Rangers, and the New York Yankees. He finished his baseball career as the senior advisor for the Tampa Bay Rays.

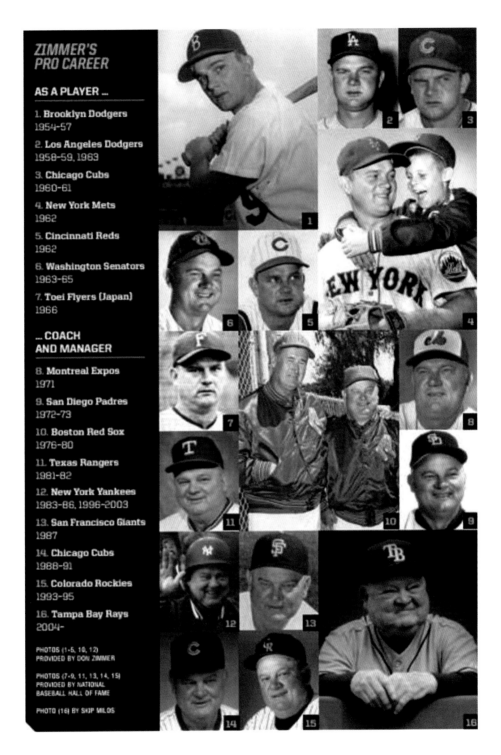

This collage documents Zim's professional career. The tenth picture shows Zim with the legendary Ted Williams of the Boston Red Sox.

Zim and Junior Gilliam

Zim was described as a *utility player*, because he played a variety of baseball positions, including second base, third base, and shortstop. He was the catcher for many games, too. Another word that describes a utility player is *versatile*.

Zim was both a dedicated athlete and a dedicated family man. Because of Soot's support, he was successful in both roles. Baseball was such a large part of Zim's life that he and Soot got married at home plate. Then, Zim changed into his uniform and played the game with Soot, in her wedding dress, rooting for him from the stands behind home plate. In that game, Zim went three for four!

A family picture of Zim, Soot, their son Tommy, and their daughter Donna in 1956

Don Zimmer, Yogi Berra, Bob Feller, and a young Derek Jeter

Zim loved the game of baseball and cherished the *camaraderie* he experienced. The lifelong friendships that he made, both on and off the field, were very special to him. Zim believed in working hard, having fun, and being a good teammate.

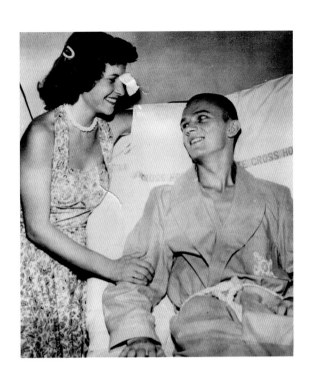
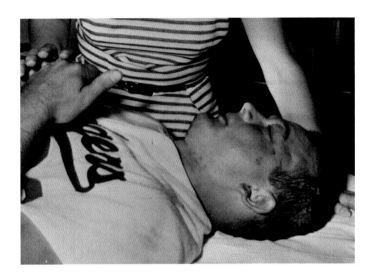

Not everything about baseball was exciting and positive for Zim. He had to *overcome adversity*. In 1953, he was hit in the head with a pitch and spent four weeks in the hospital. He needed to relearn how to walk, talk, read, and write. After Zim's beaning, Major League Baseball decided to take precautions and require that all players wear protective batting helmets. Zim was beaned again in 1956, and he fractured his cheekbone.

In 1999, when Zim was in the dugout as the bench coach for the New York Yankees, he was hit in the head with a line drive foul ball. The next day, an Army helmet was sitting on the chair by his locker to remind him to protect his head.

"If you're early,
you're never late."

– Don Zimmer

A *motto* is a sentence, phrase, or word expressing the spirit or purpose of a person. Zim had several mottos. One of them was: "What you lack in talent can be made up with desire, hustle, and giving 110 percent all of the time."

Another motto was: "If you're early, you're never late." *Punctuality* was important to Zim!

Zim was a *mentor* to younger players. He was always willing to share his knowledge of the game of baseball and how the game should be played. Occasionally, Zim would treat his players to dinner.

Zim said, "Never judge a player when he's going good. Judge him when he's going bad, and you'll find out the kind of person he really is."

Zim coaching third base and signaling plays through gestures

Zim had *veracity*, which meant that he always told the truth. He was trustworthy and dependable, which explains why people in baseball wanted to hire and work with him. Zim was an expert at predicting baseball situations and devising strategies.

Zim was a humble man. When his team won games, he credited his players for the wins instead of taking the credit himself.

Zim's baseball career took him to many places. He crisscrossed the United States from East to West and back again. Zim's baseball path led him to Alabama, California, Colorado, Florida, Illinois, Indiana, Maryland, Massachusetts, Minnesota, New York, Ohio, Tennessee, Texas, Utah, and Washington, DC.

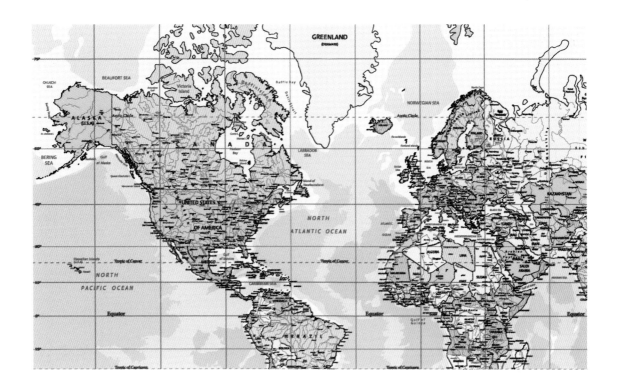

Baseball also brought Zim to other places, including Canada, Cuba, Japan, and Puerto Rico.

Zim wearing one of
his World Series rings

Zim and Jackie Robinson playing golf

Zim was a *philanthropist*! He donated his time, money, and caring spirit to others in an effort to make people's lives better. Zim visited children in hospitals. He donated some of his special baseball treasures to be raffled off to raise money for sports equipment and sports programs in various communities. Zim participated in fundraising activities and charitable events, such as golf tournaments and sports memorabilia nights. Zim's generosity *inspired* others to want to attend these events.

Always *benevolent*, Zim posed for pictures with fans, and signed autographs for them to show his appreciation for their support.

Zim signed many autographs that day.

Zim donated to All Children's Hospital in Florida, the Connecticut Sports Foundation, and Boston's Jimmy Fund. Scholarships were established in Zim's name. Baseball fields, such as the one at Griffin Park in Windham, New Hampshire, were funded through Zim's philanthropy. Thousands came out for the meet and greet for the dedication of the Don Zimmer field.

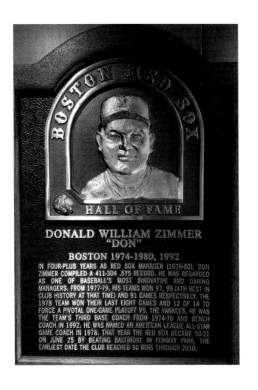

DONALD WILLIAM ZIMMER
"DON"

BOSTON 1974-1980, 1992

IN FOUR-PLUS YEARS AS RED SOX MANAGER (1976-80), DON ZIMMER COMPILED A 411-304 .575 RECORD. HE WAS REGARDED AS ONE OF BASEBALL'S MOST INNOVATIVE AND DARING MANAGERS. FROM 1977-79, HIS TEAMS WON 97, 99 (4TH BEST IN CLUB HISTORY AT THAT TIME) AND 91 GAMES RESPECTIVELY. THE 1978 TEAM WON THEIR LAST EIGHT GAMES AND 12 OF 14 TO FORCE A PIVOTAL ONE-GAME PLAYOFF VS. THE YANKEES. HE WAS THE TEAM'S THIRD BASE COACH FROM 1974-76 AND BENCH COACH IN 1992. HE WAS NAMED AN AMERICAN LEAGUE ALL-STAR GAME COACH IN 1978. THAT YEAR THE RED SOX BECAME 50-21 ON JUNE 25 BY BEATING BALTIMORE IN FENWAY PARK, THE EARLIEST DATE THE CLUB REACHED 50 WINS THROUGH 2010.

Zim was selected for many Halls of Fame around the country, including his high school Hall of Fame (Western Hills, Cincinnati, Ohio), the Greater Cincinnati High School Hall of Fame, the Brooklyn Dodgers' Hall of Fame, the Boston Red Sox Hall of Fame, and the Sports Club of Tampa Bay Hall of Fame.

Zim left a great *legacy*! He handed down his philosophy, his knowledge of baseball, and his work ethic to his *colleagues*, his players, and future generations of athletes.

Zim was a baseball legend and a *devoted* family man! He was a husband, father, grandfather, and great-grandfather.

When Don Zimmer passed away in 2014, his life was celebrated by thousands at Tropicana Field, home of the Tampa Bay Rays.

On that day, when Tampa Bay played the Seattle Mariners, both teams wore Zim's Brooklyn Dodgers uniform with his number 23 on the back of their jerseys.

Zimmer
Family Tree

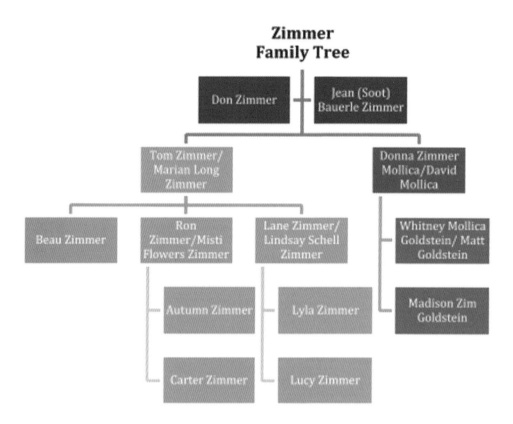

Don Zimmer | Jean (Soot) Bauerle Zimmer

Tom Zimmer/ Marian Long Zimmer

Donna Zimmer Mollica/David Mollica

Beau Zimmer

Ron Zimmer/Misti Flowers Zimmer

Lane Zimmer/ Lindsay Schell Zimmer

Whitney Mollica Goldstein/ Matt Goldstein

Autumn Zimmer

Lyla Zimmer

Madison Zim Goldstein

Carter Zimmer

Lucy Zimmer

Opening Day 2013

Athletics were important in the lives of generations of the Zimmer Family.

Tom Zimmer was a player, coach, and manager in professional baseball for many years. He signed as a catcher and infielder with the St. Louis Cardinals in 1971. In 1981, he began a forty-year career as a scout for the San Francisco Giants. Tom earned six World Series and league championship rings.

Donna Zimmer Mollica was an accomplished high school athlete in diving and cheerleading. She has been a community philanthropist throughout her adult life after retiring as a flight attendant with TWA.

As a ten-year old, Beau Zimmer was featured in a CNN children's news program called *Real News for Kids*. He went on to become a television news reporter for ABC, FOX, and CBS. Many times, he got exclusive interviews with his granddad Zim. Beau works for CBS, Tampa Bay.

Twins Ron Zimmer and Lane Zimmer were baseball and football standouts in high school. They excelled in leadership roles, and they received college academic scholarships.

Whitney Mollica Goldstein was a highly decorated softball player and student athlete in high school and college. She coached college softball at UMass Amherst, at Amherst College, and at Worcester Polytechnic Institute, where she was honored as a two-time Conference Softball Coach of the Year.

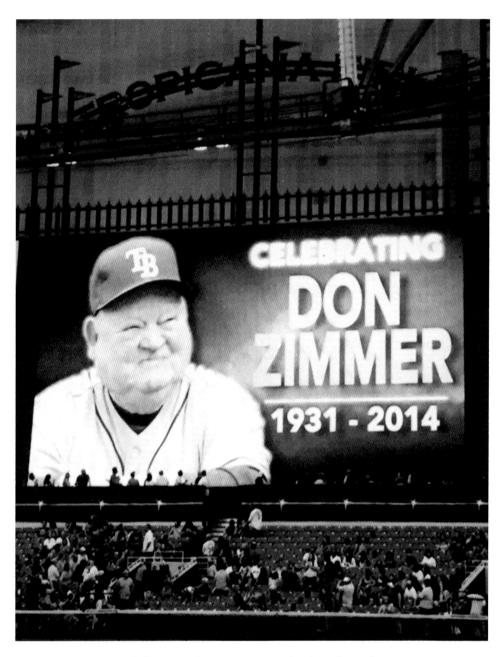

A fitting tribute to an *inspirational* man!

"Yes, our life was great and exciting, but it wasn't all peaches and cream. There was being released as a player, and firings as a manager. But we took it in stride—this was a baseball life!!"

Yes our life was great & exciting, but it wasn't all peaches & cream. There was being released as a player & firings as a manager But we took in stride, this was a baseball life.!! Love, Soot

Soot's own words best describe the Zimmers' baseball experience.